Red Kangaroo

The World's Largest Marsupial

by Natalie Lunis

Consultant: Adam Munn, Ph.D.
Faculty of Veterinary Science
The University of Sydney

BEARPORT
PUBLISHING

New York, New York

Credits

Cover, © Superstock; TOC, © Suzann Rafael Ramirez Lee/Shutterstock; 4, Kathrin Ayer; 4–5, © Owen Newman/Nature Picture Library; 6L, © Dieter Jouan & Rius/Nature Picture Library; 6R, © Auscape/Ardea; 7, © Ralph Loesche/Shutterstock; 8, © Warwick Sloss/Nature Picture Library; 9, © Mitsuaki Iwago/Minden Pictures; 10, © Jean Paul Ferrero/Ardea; 11, © blickwinkel/Alamy; 12, © Martin Harvey/Peter Arnold Inc.; 13, © Martin Harvey/DRK Photo; 14T, © Mitsuaki Iwago/Minden Pictures; 14B, © Mitsuaki Iwago/Minden Pictures; 15, © Frank Krahmer/Corbis; 16, © blickwinkel/Alamy; 17, © Owen Newman/Nature Picture Library; 18, © Simon King/npl/Minden Pictures; 19, © Jean Paul Ferrero/Ardea; 20, © Clint Scholz/iStockphoto; 21, © Martin Harvey/NHPA; 22L, © age fotostock/SuperStock; 22C, © FLPA/Alamy; 22R, © Gary Unwin/Shutterstock; 23TL, © Susan Flashman/Shutterstock; 23TR, © pamspix/iStockphoto; 23BL, © Susan Flashman/iStockphoto; 23BR, © Jan Gottwald/iStockphoto; 23BKG, © Nick Biemans/Shutterstock.

Publisher: Kenn Goin
Editorial Director: Adam Siegel
Creative Director: Spencer Brinker
Original Design: Otto Carbajal
Photo Researcher: Picture Perfect Professionals, LLC

Library of Congress Cataloging-in-Publication Data

Lunis, Natalie.
  Red kangaroo : the world's largest marsupial / by Natalie Lunis.
      p. cm. — (More supersized!)
  Includes bibliographical references and index.
  ISBN-13: 978-1-936087-24-2 (library binding)
  ISBN-10: 1-936087-24-3 (library binding)
  1. Red kangaroo—Juvenile literature. I. Title.

  QL737.M35L86 2010
  599.2'223—dc22
                                    2009030799

For more information, write to Bearport Publishing Company, Inc., 101 Fifth Avenue, Suite 6R, New York, New York 10003. Printed in the United States of America in North Mankato, Minnesota.

102009
090309CGA

10 9 8 7 6 5 4 3 2 1

Contents

King-Size Kangaroos

The red kangaroo is the biggest marsupial (mar-SOO-pee-uhl) in the world.

A male red kangaroo can weigh up to 200 pounds (91 kg).

It can stand almost seven feet (2.1 m) tall.

That's taller than most people.

Dry, Grassy Homes

Red kangaroos live in Australia.

They live on hot, dry grasslands.

The grasses that grow there are their main food.

There is very little water in the places where red kangaroos live. Luckily, the animals can survive for many days without drinking.

Red Kangaroos in the Wild

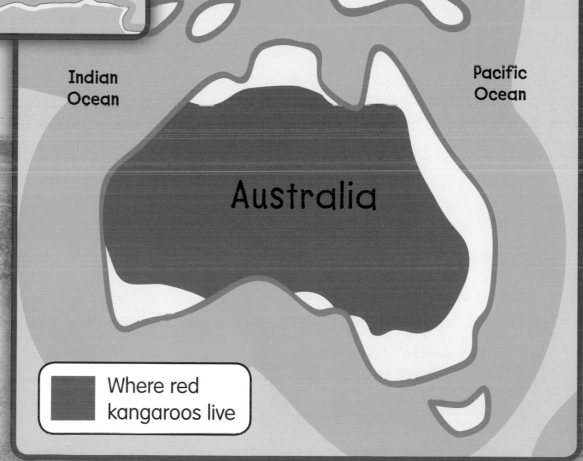

Indian Ocean

Pacific Ocean

Australia

Where red kangaroos live

Feeding Time

Red kangaroos come out to **graze** mainly in the evening and the early morning.

They bite off bunches of grass with their big front teeth.

They use their strong back teeth to chew up the grass.

During the hot daytime hours, red kangaroos rest. Sometimes they dig big holes and lie down in them to cool off.

Getting Along

Red kangaroos sometimes gather in groups called mobs.

When kangaroos meet, they usually get along.

Sometimes, however, adult males fight to decide which one is the strongest.

Most mobs are small. There are usually two to six red kangaroos in each one. However, several mobs may come together to form larger groups of up to 50 kangaroos.

kangaroos fighting

Kang-Fu Fighting

When two male kangaroos fight, they use their big back legs and their small front legs.

With their back legs, they try to land a powerful kick.

With their front legs, the animals try to scratch, hit, and wrestle each other to the ground.

The winner of the fight becomes the only male that will mate with females in the area.

back legs

During most fights, one of the kangaroos backs off and neither animal is seriously harmed.

front legs

Starting Out Tiny

About a month after mating, a female red kangaroo gives birth to a baby kangaroo, called a **joey**.

The newborn joey is tiny.

It is about one inch (2.5 cm) long, or the size of a grape.

The first thing it does is to climb into a large **pouch** on its mother's belly.

Safely inside the pouch, it drinks milk from its mother and continues to grow.

A newborn joey cannot yet see. It uses its sense of smell to find its mother's pouch.

a one-month-old joey drinking its mother's milk

a four-month-old joey inside its mother's pouch

pouch

In and Out of the Pouch

When a joey is about six months old, it leaves its mother's pouch for the first time.

It learns how to move around on the ground and gets its first taste of grass.

For the next two months, the joey starts spending more and more time out of the pouch.

Whenever it is startled or frightened, however, it jumps back in.

Finally, at the age of about eight months, the joey leaves the pouch and begins its life in the outside world.

joey

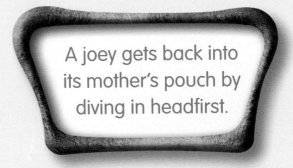

A joey gets back into its mother's pouch by diving in headfirst.

Hopping Away

Red kangaroos have only a few enemies.

Wild dogs called **dingoes** are the main animal that hunts them.

The big marsupials are quick to spot danger, however.

They are also quick to hop away.

dingoes

18

An adult red kangaroo at top speed can travel about 30 feet (9 m) in one hop. That means it can travel the length of a basketball court in three hops!

Living with People

Sometimes people in Australia have problems with red kangaroos.

The animals eat grasses and crops growing on farms and in gardens.

Australians are trying to find ways to live with the furry creatures, however.

After all, red kangaroos are important to their country.

When most people think of Australia, they think of the big, hopping animals that live there—and nowhere else in the world!

In Australia, people in cars and trucks sometimes hit kangaroos. To cut down on accidents, some places have signs to warn drivers that kangaroos may be crossing.

More Big Marsupials

Red kangaroos belong to a group of animals called marsupials. All marsupials are mammals—animals that are warm-blooded, have hair or fur, and drink milk from their mothers early in life. Unlike other mammals, a marsupial grows and stays safe in a pouch on its mother's belly after it is born.

Here are three more big marsupials.

Eastern Gray Kangaroo

The eastern gray kangaroo is the second-largest marsupial in the world. A gray kangaroo can weigh 187 pounds (85 kg) and stand 6.5 feet (2 m) tall.

Antilopine Wallaroo

Wallaroos are another kind of kangaroo. They can weigh up to 132 pounds (60 kg) and stand more than 5 feet (1.5 m) tall.

Southern Hairy-Nosed Wombat

This marsupial is not a kind of kangaroo. It can weigh 79 pounds (36 kg) and be 28 inches (71 cm) tall.

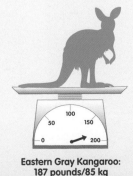

Red Kangaroo: 200 pounds/91 kg

Eastern Gray Kangaroo: 187 pounds/85 kg

Antilopine Wallaroo: 132 pounds/60 kg

Southern Hairy-Nosed Wombat: 79 pounds/36 kg

Glossary

dingoes
(DING-ohz)
wild dogs that live
in Australia

joey
(JOH-ee)
a baby kangaroo

graze
(GRAYZ)
to eat grass

pouch
(POUCH)
the pocket-like
part of a mother
kangaroo's belly
used for carrying
her young

Index

Read More

Levine, Michelle. *Jumping Kangaroos.* Minneapolis, MN: Lerner (2005).

Marsico, Katie. *A Kangaroo Joey Grows Up.* New York: Children's Press (2007).

Noonan, Diana. *The Kangaroo.* Philadelphia: Chelsea House (2003).

Learn More Online

To learn more about red kangaroos, visit
www.bearportpublishing.com/MoreSuperSized